XTREME RAPTORS

★ ★ ★ ★

EAGLES

BY

S.L. HAMILTON

A&D Xtreme
An imprint of Abdo Publishing | abdopublishing.com

abdopublishing.com

Published by Abdo Publishing, a division of ABDO, PO Box 398166, Minneapolis, Minnesota 55439. Copyright ©2018 by Abdo Consulting Group, Inc. International copyrights reserved in all countries. No part of this book may be reproduced in any form without written permission from the publisher. A&D Xtreme™ is a trademark and logo of Abdo Publishing.

Printed in the United States of America, North Mankato, Minnesota.
022017
052017

THIS BOOK CONTAINS RECYCLED MATERIALS

Editor: John Hamilton
Graphic Design: Sue Hamilton
Cover Design: Candice Keimig
Cover Photo: iStock
Interior Photos: Alamy-pg 20; AP-pg 4-5; DCEggWatch-pg 26 (inset); Francesco Veronesi-pg 29 (bottom right); iStock-pgs 1, 2-3, 6, 10, 11, 12-15, 21 (left), 26 & 32; Minden Pictures-pgs 7, 8, 9, 16, 17, 18 (bottom), 21 (right), 22-23, 24, 25, 27, 28, & 30-31; Philippe Verbelen-pg 29 (bottom left); Science Source-pg 19 (eagle skeleton); Shoestring Travelers-pg 29 (top); Shreeram (Wikimedia)-pg 18 (top); & U.S. Fish and Wildlife-pg 14 (feathers chart).

Websites
To learn more about Raptors, visit abdobooklinks.com. These links are routinely monitored and updated to provide the most current information available.

Publisher's Cataloging-in-Publication Data

Names: Hamilton, S. L., author.
Title: Eagles / by S. L. Hamilton.
Description: Minneapolis, MN : Abdo Publishing, 2018. |
Series: Xtreme raptors
      Includes index.
Identifiers: LCCN 2016962217 | ISBN 9781532110016 (lib. bdg.) |
      ISBN 9781680787863 (ebook)
Subjects: LCSH: Eagles--Juvenile literature.
Classification: DDC 598.9/42--dc23
LC record available at http://lccn.loc.gov/2016962217

CONTENTS

EAGLES

Eagles are big and powerful birds of prey. These raptors, or meat eaters, are fierce hunters and fiendish scavengers. They track and catch their meals using their amazing eyesight, or they steal from other predators.

Bald Eagle (*Haliaeetus leucocephalus*)

 XTREME FACT – The bald eagle was chosen as a symbol for the United States in 1782. The eagle was picked because of its proud look, great strength, and long life.

An eagle's sharp eyes, powerful talons, and large, hooked beak make it a predator to be respected. Armies as far back as the Roman Empire have used this fierce raptor as a symbol of strength and power. Sports teams, cars, ships, military vehicles, and even a spacecraft have been named for the mighty eagle.

SPECIES

There are 68 eagle species in the world. The greatest varieties are found in Africa, Europe, and Asia. Only golden eagles and bald eagles make their homes in North America. Alaska has the largest eagle population on the continent.

SEA EAGLE

Bald Eagle
(*Haliaeetus leucocephalus*)

BOOTED EAGLE

Golden Eagle
(*Aquila chrysaetos*)

XTREME FACT – A bald eagle's Latin name, *Haliaeetus leucocephalus*, means "white-headed sea eagle." In times past, the word "bald" once meant "white" or "white-faced."

Eagle species are divided into four general groups: sea eagles, booted eagles, snake eagles, and harpy eagles. Sea eagles eat mainly fish. Booted eagles have feathers down to their ankles. Snake eagles feed on reptiles. Harpy eagles live in tropical forests and are some of the largest eagles on Earth.

SNAKE EAGLE

Black-Chested Snake Eagle *(Circaetus pectoralis)*

HARPY EAGLE

Harpy Eagle *(Harpia harpyja)*

HABITAT & PREY

Eagles live on all continents except Antarctica. These raptors live near their prey. Many eagles eat fish as a main part of their diet. They are often found near lakes, rivers, and streams.

Bald Eagle
(*Haliaeetus leucocephalus*)

XTREME FACT – *Bald eagles regurgitate, or throw up, the indigestible parts of their food, such as fur, feathers, and bones.*

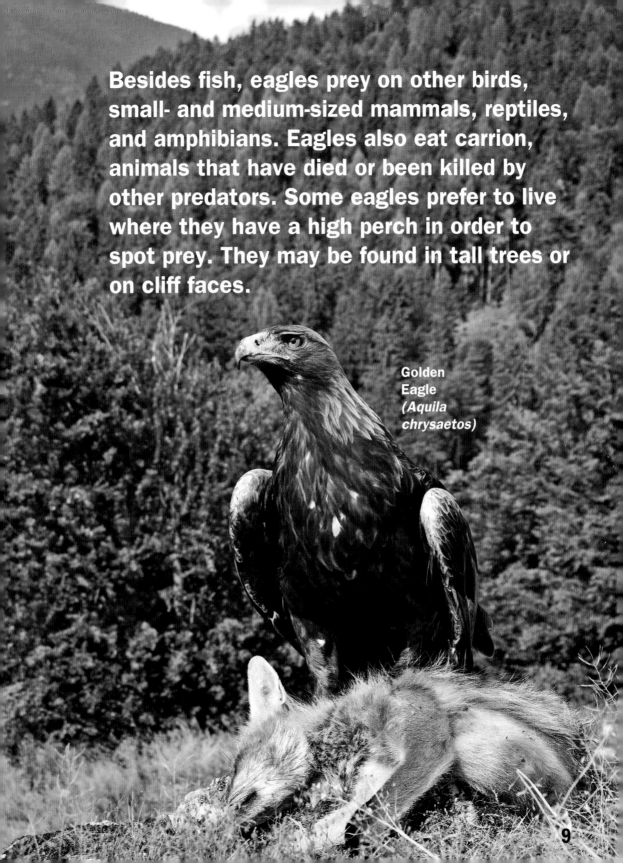

Besides fish, eagles prey on other birds, small- and medium-sized mammals, reptiles, and amphibians. Eagles also eat carrion, animals that have died or been killed by other predators. Some eagles prefer to live where they have a high perch in order to spot prey. They may be found in tall trees or on cliff faces.

Golden Eagle (*Aquila chrysaetos*)

EYESIGHT

Eagles have excellent vision during the day. They can see four or five times farther than an average human. When the sun is up, these diurnal hunters can see prey moving up to two miles (3.2 km) away. Eagles have "binocular vision." Their forward-facing eyes allow them to accurately judge distances. They see objects very clearly and in bright colors.

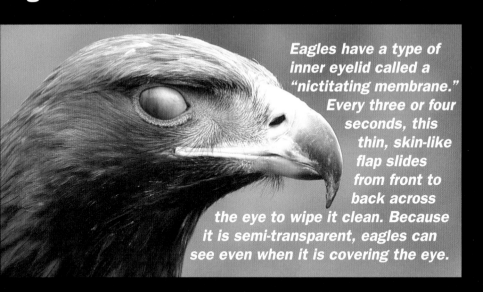

Eagles have a type of inner eyelid called a "nictitating membrane." Every three or four seconds, this thin, skin-like flap slides from front to back across the eye to wipe it clean. Because it is semi-transparent, eagles can see even when it is covering the eye.

XTREME FACT – A person with the vision of an eagle could spot a tiny ant on the ground from the top of a 10-story building.

BEAKS

An eagle's beak is sharp and curved. It is made to tear off pieces of meat from its prey. The beak continues to grow all of the eagle's life. To trim and clean its beak, an eagle performs an action called "feaking." After eating, the raptor rubs its beak on stones or other sharp surfaces.

XTREME FACT – Beaks are covered in hard layers of keratin, the same material in human fingernails.

WINGS & FEATHERS

An individual eagle has about 7,000 feathers. Some are colorful to attract a mate. Others keep the bird warm. But its flight feathers, or "primaries," on the wings and tail, are very strong. These strong feathers, combined with an eagle's powerful wing muscles, let the raptor fly for long periods of time as it hunts for food. The fierce bird can sometimes even carry prey weighing more than itself.

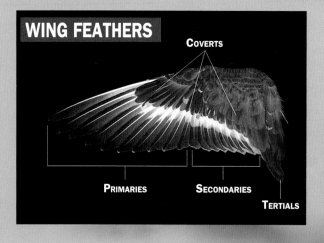

WING FEATHERS

COVERTS

PRIMARIES

SECONDARIES

TERTIALS

XTREME FACT – If an eagle's wings get too wet while fishing, it may not be able to lift off from the water's surface. It can use its wings as "oars," rowing itself across the water, fish in its talons, until it gets to land. The eagle can eat its lunch while its wings dry off.

White-Tailed Eagle
(*Haliaeetus albicilla*)

LEGS, FEET & TALONS

Eagles use their feet and talons to capture prey. Each foot is "anisodactylous." This means it has three toes in front and one in back. The three front talons curve toward the back. The single back talon curves to the front. This allows the long, sharp talons to wrap around prey.

Most eagles have scaly legs. The scales protect them from attacks by prey. Golden eagles are different. Feathers cover their entire legs. The feathers help protect the raptors from the cold.

Golden Eagle
(*Aquila chrysaetos*)

XTREME FACT – Eagles are thieves. They steal fish and other prey from birds, animals, and even humans. Eagles also eat roadkill. This causes eagle injuries and deaths when the scavengers are struck by passing vehicles.

SMALLEST EAGLES

South Nicobar Serpent Eagle (*Spilornis klossi*)

The smallest eagle is the South Nicobar serpent eagle (*Spilornis klossi*). It weighs about one pound (.45 kg) and is 16 inches (41 cm) in length. It is found in forests on islands off the coast of India. Although small, it is a fierce hunter. Its prey includes reptiles, rats, and birds.

Little eagles (*Hieraaetus morphnoides*) live in Australia and New Guinea. These small raptors weigh about one pound (.45 kg) and are 18 inches (46 cm) long. They prey on rabbits and other small mammals, birds, and lizards.

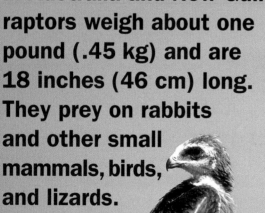

Little Eagle (*Hieraaetus morphnoides*)

NORTH AMERICAN EAGLES — SIZE COMPARISON

Of North America's two species of eagles, bald eagles are slightly larger than golden eagles.

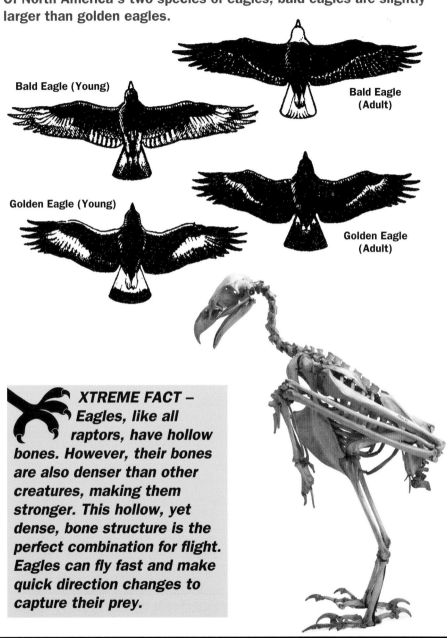

Bald Eagle (Young)

Bald Eagle (Adult)

Golden Eagle (Young)

Golden Eagle (Adult)

XTREME FACT – Eagles, like all raptors, have hollow bones. However, their bones are also denser than other creatures, making them stronger. This hollow, yet dense, bone structure is the perfect combination for flight. Eagles can fly fast and make quick direction changes to capture their prey.

Largest Eagles

The Philippine eagle (*Pithecophaga jefferyi*) is the largest eagle in the world in terms of length and wing surface. It grows up to 3.3 feet (1 m) in length, with a wingspan of more than 7 feet (2 m). A Philippine eagle may weigh more than 17 pounds (7.7 kg). It is found in the forests of the Philippines.

Philippine Eagle
(*Pithecophaga jefferyi*)

Steller's Sea Eagle (*Haliaeetus pelagicus*)

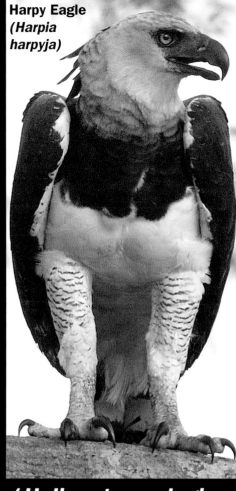

Harpy Eagle (*Harpia harpyja*)

The Steller's sea eagle (*Haliaeetus pelagicus*) and the harpy eagle (*Harpia harpyja*) are largest in weight. The Steller's sea eagle is found along the coast of northeastern Asia. The harpy eagle is the largest raptor found in the Americas. It lives in the rainforests of Central and South America. Both of these eagles may weigh up to 20 pounds (9 kg).

Golden Eagle
(Aquila chrysaetos)

FASTEST EAGLES

The golden eagle is the fastest flier among eagles. By using its powerful wings, it can fly up to 80 mph (129 kph). It can reach a dive speed of up to 200 miles per hour (322 kph).

XTREME FACT – To prove himself a worthy partner during courtship, a male golden eagle may grab a stone, carry it up in the air, drop it, then dive at a death-defying speed to catch the stone before it hits the ground.

UNIQUE MEALS

Most eagles prefer to eat fish. However, depending on an eagle's size and where it lives, eagles hunt for other prey. They eat mammals, reptiles, and even carrion. The Philippine eagle is also known as the monkey-eating eagle. The martial eagle (*Polemaetus bellicosus*) of Kenya, Africa, eats mongooses and antelopes.

A martial eagle (*Polemaetus bellicosus*) eats a banded mongoose.

Golden Eagle
(*Aquila chrysaetos*)

In Greece, golden eagles eat turtle meat. Eagles also eat snakes. If a venomous snake manages to bite the eagle and inject its poison, the eagle will die. To protect itself, the raptor keeps the snake's fangs away from its body.

A crested serpent eagle
(*Spilornis cheela*) eats a snake.

NESTING

Eagles build huge nests using sticks, tree boughs, bones, antlers, grasses, leaves, and other materials they find.

Eagle Nest

Nests are placed high on cliffs, trees, and even human-made towers. Eagles reuse their nests, adding more material each year. An average nest is up to 6 feet (1.8 m) wide and 4 feet (1.2 m) deep.

 XTREME FACT – The largest recorded bird's nest was built by bald eagles in Florida. It was 9 feet 6 inches (2.9 m) wide and 20 feet (6.1 m) deep.

A bald eagle feeds a chick.

Eagles lay one to three eggs each year. Both eagle parents stay with the nest until their chicks "fledge." This is when the young have developed large enough feathers to fly.

A fledgling bald eagle exercises its wings as it prepares to fly.

ARE THEY ENDANGERED?

Bald eagles were listed as "endangered" in 1967 in the United States. This was due to habitat loss and poisons in the environment. But with new laws and careful protection, bald eagle populations slowly grew. They were upgraded to "threatened" in 1995 and finally taken off the threatened list in 2007. Laws continue to protect eagles today.

XTREME FACT – DDT was a chemical product used to kill mosquitoes and other insects in the 1940s and 1950s. But DDT got into water supplies and then into fish. When female bald eagles ate the fish, the chemical caused their eggshells to break easily. By the 1960s, few eaglets were born. After this was discovered, DDT use was banned in 1972.

There are some eagles that are nearly extinct in the wild. These "critically endangered" species include the Philippine eagle, the Flores hawk eagle, and the Madagascar fish eagle. Many people work to keep these species, and all eagles, from dying out.

Philippine Eagle
(Pithecophaga jefferyi)

Flores Hawk Eagle
(Nisaetus floris)

Madagascar Fish Eagle
(Haliaeetus vociferoides)

GLOSSARY

BIRDS OF PREY
Birds that eat meat. Birds of prey are also known as raptors.

CARRION
The dead flesh of animals that are decaying.

DIURNAL
Creatures that are active during the day.

ENDANGERED
When there are so few numbers of a plant or animal, it is close to becoming extinct. See also "Threatened."

EXTINCT
When every member of a specific living thing has died. Dinosaurs are extinct.

HABITAT
The natural home of a living thing.

PREDATOR
An animal that hunts, kills, and eats other animals.

ROMAN EMPIRE
The ancient civilization centered in Rome, in present-day Italy. The Roman Empire began in 27 BC and lasted for hundreds of years. Led by a series of emperors who held great power, the Roman Empire at its height stretched over most of Europe, plus large sections of northern Africa and western Asia.

SCAVENGER
Creatures that eat what they can find, including dead and dying prey.

SPECIES
A group of plants or animals that are related to one another. They look alike and may produce offspring.

THREATENED
When a plant or animal is at risk of extinction in the very near future. See also "Endangered."

VENOM
A poisonous liquid that some reptiles, such as snakes, use for killing prey and for defense.

INDEX